TACT

LILY DUFFY

TACT ©2021 by **Lily Duffy**. Published in the United States by Vegetarian Alcoholic Press. Not one part of this work may be reproduced without expressed written consent from the author. For more information, please contact vegalpress@gmail.com

Cover art & design by Kevin Barrett Kane

CONTENTS

7

Gratis

31

Vials on Earth

51

The Shame Suite

59

Awning

67

Problems in Walking at Night

77

Grommet: An Address

GRATIS

In being untoward to him I have moved him

Or, how I core myself out of a contract over

The bellowing of houses very actual

On a wall two shadows appear and water

Screams through the pipes

Sometimes, it really is as if I am two—the neighbor coughing and spitting on his patio for a combined half of every hour, which, from inside our house at the opposite end, I can hear as if I'm sitting right beside him, and I am mad, distracted, disgusted, but then someone entirely *else* comes in feeling sad, sorry, forgiving, and when that *else* enters I think, *yes, of course*, and after that, cannot remember feeling any other way, forget there are other ways to feel.

♦

His hand goes clockwise on the small of my back, will rub the same

spot same direction until I reach behind and pull it away, an

agreement to hold it in mine. At weddings, I imagine the back

of my folding chair as an installation, a square of slinky fabric and his hand

a body pleasuring itself—wonder if anyone behind us wants

to slap it away.

Every girl is born with a store

                                                inside her. To make her responsive to hands.

What would her hands feel like

                                                if they belonged to someone else? How would

she know?

"Neither of us said anything for a long time and then we both said everything at the same time. After that, there was nothing left to say"

There'd been a mole on his left temple for as long as I'd known him, and he suddenly began covering it up. First with a cheap stick of concealer kept in the medicine cabinet, several shades too light with a dry, chalky texture that made it nearly impossible to blend, resulting in an ironic highlighting effect. Soon he was applying it to the skin beneath his eyes which gave him the look of a beach bum, dazed and symmetrical. When I asked what he was using he first pretended not to know what I meant, but soon grew flustered by my silence; said he'd been using a new shampoo, said he suspected his skin might be sensitive to it, but his hair did look thicker, didn't it, and he did really love the smell.

"How soon do you feel like you need to take this offer?"
A caught moon figures it out
Right now he asks about our future, right now he does
Mainly the parlor
Books for babies
A book that's a lozenge for the baby I'll wear like a breast plate
As I deliver my speech
He asks about my "timeline," wants to make a list
He starts a list
He has a question

◆

Wine at the party, so what
"Forgot" we had somewhere to be later
Am I tacky?
Doesn't matter, doesn't
Cancel dinner, does it
All these calls taking themselves

"Sooner rather than later, obviously?"

Lights out

My hands all over the county

Understood,

My waist singing inward

Tends to itself, isn't locked or

Sinking an answer

The fourth wall is my face. It has a door, or sometimes doesn't, a balance

of zero, concern for the public, and when that little light starts to blink, that means

we're done.

                                                  This hour, it has to go

                                                  We've had it

                                                  Now it has to go

I know it sounds crazy, he said, talking to my stomach (a taunt in response to an earlier request that he ejaculate inside me—something done about that)

A dress I had was a bond. Night bent around it

The portraits we took on the lawn

I at half-bawl. Put myself *inside* the trellis—you know, him holding *us*

He whimpered until his mother took off her skirt suit

The father wore her dickey like a headscarf, shook his keys in our faces and did "crazy person eyes"

I held up my rake. Air coiled around it

Drapes and tassels, floor plans and swatches

When the shoot ended I was doing "That's him pretending to be her"

He watched the whole thing on his phone—his red ear

Years ago he began wearing my perfume. Half-retaliating, and also not wanting to smell like him, I began wearing his cologne. We maintain the arrangement. Still, when the bottles run out, he buys the cologne and I the perfume, though neither of us have worn what we've bought since the switch. We each leave our bottle on top of the dresser—not touching it after that—and watch the liquid disappear. There've also been a few times I was doing laundry and found a skirt or top I didn't remember wearing in the hamper, and then I smelled it. Not a word between us about it, any of it.

One theory is there's a shelf in my stomach, one that holds his ingredients, and he's

                                                              trying to get to the shelf

Finished dinner on the stairs—why had I done that?

A kind of noble tripping a shadow does to pass the mess, funny-angry

"Safe in the time-out spot?" He cleared his plate, chuckling

Then locked himself in the basement

Clinking forkfuls of meat and skin, gulping water for air

To be "shelved"—to be of no use at the present moment, and so put away for later (with the presumption that "it" will "keep" until needed)

I imagine opening a closet to find a spill of hair overtop a dress overtop a pair of shoes

In my dream, he told me all about me

You're being very loud

                                           But now I've acknowledged you

                                           And think it would be better

                                           If we talked about that

                                           As a family

So what I'm going to do

                                           Is go back into our room

                                           And put on that outfit

                                           Then we're going to come out

                                           To hear what you have to say

A knock implicates a door

Loud so as to scare you.

We eat at a restaurant that serves red food exclusively. I get the strawberry lobster and he the prime rib, served shaved in a beet balsamic reduction. Our food comes on red, edible plates (baked apple syrup) served by a waiter in a red fedora who addresses us as *M'Lord* and *M'Lady,* though the ambience suggests this is not obligatory, possibly even discouraged. Everything is exquisite. We're waiting on our dessert, a malted raspberry-fig risotto to share, when he asks a question: *Couldn't you have worn a red dress? You knew we were coming to a red foods restaurant. It would've been nice.* I lift the cruet of cranberry vinaigrette off the table and pop the stopper, dressing myself chest-down in bright liquid. The fabric of my dress (chartreuse with tiny black flowers) turns more purple than red and I am pleased, sipping my wine. The waiter brings our risotto and gushes apologies, blotting my chest with her apron, offering a frock from the lost and found. I thank her sweetly but decline, dabbing my neckline with a napkin. She scampers off and I turn my gaze to him: flat-faced and glassy-eyed, rigid in his seat. I reach for my spoon, smiling, the corners of my mouth going out instead of up. He does not have any risotto.

"How, when listening to him, do you feel?"

"Huge and dumb. Slow and shitting myself. A little bit blind."

"Do you think, in reality, that you're any of those things?"

"Sometimes. It depends."

"What does it depend on?"

"If I'm being him or not."

"And when are you him?"

"When I can't be her."

When he reached out and touched my face, I grew

angry. Could feel his

hands were unwashed.

Mealtime governed us. He'd ignore the knife to his left, fork-stabbing the thigh before lifting it whole to his mouth and tearing off a bite. I cut mine into cubes, dragging the knife across the plate to emphasize the act, a shrill admonishment (hoping he'd admonish back; never once). Allowed the tendons in my neck to stiffen as I chewed, envisioning the meat as a conflict to pulverize, a threat that squirmed at the back of my throat. Swallowing became an act of disposal. He disliked the labor of chewing and performed it sparingly, requiring him to gulp, pause, and pound his chest 'til the body gave way. I tried but could not digest these moments. Chunks of gristle that flew across the room and were found days or weeks later. I began collections I dreamt of revealing to him in an epiphanic sequence, but after one particular dream where I arranged the gristles into a sigil on his dashboard, I woke to the sound of blood pumping through my head. Dumped the gristles in a plastic bag and disposed of it at a convenience store; downed a milkshake in the blasting heat before driving home. A small mourning apportioned.

Called him a "shit ass" last night, dreamt the word   all over the bed

It was like nothing to say it—a catch of keys, car
                               brought around the back

        Inside the head, various mats: days, words, getting touched, lists for what's done or needed

The glad-singing voices of neighbors   I shred, add to the pyre
                        Glowing songs of work and weather, children and spouses
The mouth is sleepless, even in sleep. I imagine the future   arriving each day
                                                                   like the mail
              This life is a good life and I need nothing
                                       but the sky above me, the leaves
under my feet   which alert me to my movements and double them

Given the choice, I leave the body behind in a denim jumper embroidered with flowers

A slab of meat   more tender   with his hand upon it

Babies reading inside me

Breathe in order to sleep in order to read

Through me

♦

And when their eyes close, they see legs

A question becomes obvious once it takes on your shape.

Courier that I was when I was screaming from the shower.

Definite head on the table. Rises as the steam rolls in.

On the subject of generosity: dozing while someone tells

their story of being made. He made several deposits and motioned

for me to stand, kneeling under me to watch for returns.

I wanted nothing with eyes to witness me. I laid in bed

surrounded by weed and sour candy, letting the cat scratch

at the door. Wore a coat always, shoes ready on the floor at the foot

of the mattress. Counted the matches in the box, marked my

calendar in pen, lit a candle. Superstition as a way of holding the body

accountable to the life.

"If you could wake up and have a whole new life—and you didn't have to worry about cutting ties, or other logistics—what would it look like?"

"Quiet. Private—I think I'd want to be around people a lot, but they wouldn't touch or talk to me unless I wanted them to. I'd want to make things for them."

"What kinds of things would you want to make?"

"I don't know…art, I guess. I keep thinking about these little manuals, but they'd be from the perspective of the object—like, how to change a car's oil, but it's the car telling you how. That sounds cutesy, but it'd be more about listening."

"Interesting. It sounds like you've already thought about this quite a bit."

"Yeah."

"What do you think it might take for you to get to that life?"

"I don't know."

Serums	Tides	Creams
Serums	Serums	Bulbs
Tides	Serums	Tides
Serums	Creams	Tides
Bulbs	Bulbs	Tides
Creams	Tides	Tides

I was laughing. I'd begun much too soon the drinking and then I was laughing. I spat something up and turned my head—rid of it before even the action. I trusted myself despite my state. It was of course night.

Not so much a choice as a method, not so much a method as a knack

For those who will card me, look at my card, then ask—

I was tired, and going somewhere I could sleep

He wrote in his report that I was using his badge "like a mirror" as he spoke to me

They had me put my hair up for the picture

♦

The theme was "holiday"

Perfume running down my asscrack

Is how you feel "the truth?"

                              A stain is my work. The voice is shrill. I can sleep through it.

Or a scent arriving

in lines from the door

makes way for your head

A rash on my neck that spread to my eyelids

The immediate thought: a homeless man I'd shook hands with days before

Guilt rushing like blood to the head

Outside of sleep, a body's an occupation. You don't just "have" a life

Some boys on a bridge want my scarf. I tell them it's theirs if they can guess my name

The error of the "bath bomb" (grain and mint)

Began sleeping with the face wrapped in plastic (a hole for the mouth). Dropped all my creams and was "hanging in"

Neck to eyelids, eyelids to wrists—the skin hotter with the hot eye on it. The eye the most hot

My smile's a glare that's charred from wanting

At the gas station, a woman pulls up beside a pump, gets out of her car, unscrews the cap, bends down, and begins vomiting into her gas tank. Vomit slides down the wheel well and pools on the ground, the whole ordeal lasting several minutes. When she's finished, she wipes her mouth with the back of her wrist, gets back in her car and starts it. Sits there for several minutes, applying makeup in the mirror of her sun visor, before driving away.

Thirty minutes in front of a mirror trying to "wing" my eyeliner—the pen's gone dry and I have to recap it. The damage: an entire travel pack of cotton swabs in the trash, tipped with black. Raw red circles at the outer corner of each eye, lids pink and flaking (the rash still healing). Too painful to stay open, I realize. Asleep by eight.

At nine, I smelled like plasticky strawberries

At ten, poison and scalp

At fourteen, fruit punch on the neck, cherries and almonds on the legs

At sixteen, warm vanilla sugar

At nineteen, musky oranges left on a grill

At twenty, marshmallows and blunts

At twenty-two, other people

At twenty-four, maple syrup, or cologne, or a filing cabinet

At twenty-five, skin

A cruel game some guys came up with during a party I was at, wherein all the girls "who had nothing to hide" washed their makeup off and lined up for the men to evaluate them individually before convening to come up with a collective "order"—Most Different Looking (ugliest) to Least Different Looking (prettiest), which they would communicate to the female participants by physically moving them into that order before announcing which end of the line was which. Particularly cruel about the game were the circumstances surrounding it—everyone was drunk (no driving home), the temperature outside was below freezing (no walking home), it was late in a very rural part of the county (no calling a cab), and any girl who'd gotten a higher (uglier) ranking knew she couldn't put her makeup back on without risking teasing that, given the circumstances, she didn't have the emotional faculties to withstand at that time. Particularly sad about that night is that if all the girls had trusted each other enough to know that, even drunk, none of us actually wanted to partake, the game never would have taken place, and the short girl at the unfortunate end of the line (who was actually sort of pretty and really didn't look all that different without makeup, and almost certainly did not look the *most* different without it of all of us; rather, she was just the chubbiest) wouldn't have felt like she had to let out an awful, forced laugh when we could all feel the sharp air she was taking in through her nose, in order to protect herself from further humiliation, and the face of the girl next to her wouldn't have gone disturbingly vacant, nor would the girl at the opposite end of the line yelling, in a voice much higher than her normal one, that it was "shot time" be the thing that allowed the rest of us to feel like we were physically capable of breaking from the shape we'd been fashioned into. After that night, I wore considerably less makeup, to parties and in general, and pretended to be convinced that something positive had come out of the experience. The girl whose face looked like she'd abandoned it got a tattoo a couple weeks later—it said "Beauty is in the eye of the beholder" in green cursive across her stomach. She has several kids now, and when I saw her at a friend's baby shower a few months back, I was ashamed of the strong desire I had to ask if I could see it again.

"They had a real cloud over the stage and it followed this little girl; she ran into the fake well face-first trying to escape it. Now she has a scar where that soft divot between her neck and collarbone is."

Find the plastic for my

Face on the floor every morning, after

I've slipped on it

Woke on the breakfast window seat, phoneless and wet

Now to collect:

shoes   (deep end of pool)

wallet   (lodged in bra's left cup)

keys   (hooked to the belt of a sleeping stranger)

phone   (missing)

Checking the bathroom when I notice I've been scratching my palm all morning. I look down at it—in smeared black ink: **LAUNDRY**

In the basement, buzzing at the bottom of a hamper (mosses of the grown). Palm red for the rest of the day

Titanium Dioxide 15.0%, Zinc Oxide 10.0%. Inactive Ingredients: Mica, Tricaprylin, Boron Nitride, Zinc Stearate, Lauroyl Lysine, Calcium Aluminum Borosilicate, Camellia Oleifera Leaf Extract, Chamomilla Recutita (Matricaria) Flower Extract, Ginkgo Biloba Leaf Extract, Panax Ginseng Root Extract, Carthamus Tinctorius (Safflower) Seed Oil, Tocopheryl Acetate, Retinyl Palmitate, Ascorbyl Palmitate, Chlorphenesin, Potassium Sorbate, Sodium Dehydroacetate. May Contain: Iron Oxides, Titanium Dioxide.

Bought: the thinking being that nineteen ingredients seems a modest amount, particularly for a cosmetic (bronzing powder) not advertised as "natural" or "organic," which, in the case of makeup, can often compromise the product's consistency, and, in turn, its application and finish. In any event, it's spring again, and tonight I will wear this bronzing powder as instructed ("apply to all the places where the sun hits your face," which I read as "all the places where your face protrudes") with the question that accompanies the application of any new product to my face: *what will the face say?*

There were booths for the face—paints and clays, photos and plasters

Hats for the drinks and drinkers, a coat check for keys, credit cards for bonds

I bought a funnel cake iced with buttercream and ate it on a hay bale

Behind me, a handmade sign over a pile of vomit: **FREE**. Hot dog floating in the toilet

Here, every body parties—arrives to trash and becomes "trashed"

The purpose being to clear one of one's self, to make room again

A woman sits in a chair that separates a man and his preteen son in the waiting room of a doctor's office. She is dressed in a gray pantsuit and shiny black heels; her purse looks expensive and her makeup accentuates her prominent cheekbones. From her skin she looks to be a redhead or a strawberry blonde, but it's impossible to verify, as her eyebrows have been painted with a bright red liquid the consistency of tempera, her short hair slicked back with it. After a few minutes, a door opens and her name is called; she follows a nurse in and the door closes slowly behind her. Thirty minutes later, the door opens and the woman walks out—her head and eyebrows have been shaved off, and she is beaming. Her phone rings as she's leaving the office, and she answers it with a squeak accompanied by tiny vibrating hops.

Nothing sounds good. Worse, the woman I've imagined has grown a bite on her face from which she drinks and the world's question is, *do you think she likes it?*

Though the real question is perhaps not if she likes it, but if she'll get in the car—so much a question it's become a study; federally sponsored sedans that pull up beside her at least twice an hour.

I have a problem. Here's my problem: when engaging with someone and enjoying myself, my face sometimes deadens. Goes completely slack.

Mortified: to die from humiliation, or, the condition of being permanently embarrassed of one's own death.

"She jumped neatly like a pin of flesh into a pool of water"

THE SHAME SUITE

The face has often felt

It owns nothing.

Says:

I am so young. Everything moves across me. I receive my weather from the elements of both worlds, and I sense when I am seen. Reaction is my living. The one who lives through me believes she is me, and this is the first act of self-betrayal.

The problem breathes and holds certain

Fantasies accountable, spread like frost

Across streets, houses, bouts of excess

Product application or pale gardening. Thickens the dream

Standing by the door in his hotel room, he looks me in my eyes and reaches out to touch a large, bleeding pimple on my chin. Wipes the blood with his thumb, his thumb on his pants. I am steps behind, the thumb stuck, imprinting itself on my face (the pimple gains a heartbeat). His eyes slightly wet, mine pounding. The hair on his face edged sharply, a little graphic, but—his eyes are kind.

This poem's got a naturally-occurring cleft in it where I might turn, if I could, away from its narrative. It takes place in an irregularly-shaped room, roughly 20 x 15, with a table by the door. On the table, a modern cornucopia spills chips, nuts, and granola bars; fruit snacks and drink packets, all trailing to a badge with his name on it (a silent request that it be examined (turned around several times in the mouth) before spoken). Across from the table is a window facing an icy courtyard with a birdbath at its center, crumbling like no bird's ever touched it. The toilet's running, been running since I got here. When I ask him if he's called about it, he says he doesn't hear it, that that's *just the way toilets sound* in his experience.

I drop him off at the university where he will attend a conference with a smear of blood and pus near the crotch of his khakis. 37 days later, when we meet in a hotel room in another city, he sucks the spot where the pimple had been; I fly home with a mark in the shape of his mouth on my chin.

"I like your nose

—your *big* nose"

"You're loud and proud. It's hot, it's very attractive"

"I did wonder about your ethnicity. I had some ideas"

"If someone made a silhouette of you, there'd be no mistaking"

"It does possess a sort of nobility"

"I'm sure you've been told it's a flaw, but to me, it's beautiful"

"Irish? Not with that schnoz!"

"I thought you were Jewish when I saw you. Because of your

(gestures toward his own face with index and middle fingers diverting)

"—eyes"

I feel most beautiful in fall, at which point I sense my soul drop

Like a veil over my face

"I am my own friend"

The thought insane, muscular, growing out of me like a limb

I sit immediately down to eat. Mouth opens, emits a sound like something husked

An interest in common names with unusual spellings—"Krystina," for example, exists less when heard, more when written

She's wearing a mask when she answers the door, eyes crinkled; someone's sick

As you speak with a person, you might notice you're surrounded by some type of debris. Might notice yourself playing with it

I was singing to a crowd of crying family members in a parking lot. Then, I opened my eyes, said the clerk, polishing a tomato on his shirted belly before passing it into the bag

I often think of myself as being "wrung." As in:

You tell me I'm tired, but actually, I'm angry.

I'm going to rub your back and stroke your hair until you sleep.

AWNING

I love a felled—

Goes the phrase.

Woke with gels, the word, the beyond-word

I talked to him because I was afraid if I didn't he'd forget me

(squeezes temples so the jaw slacks)

He slid his hand down my pants and patted me

(laughs a clipped laugh)

Woke later with scratches (knew of course it'd gone beyond patting, but the patting's what I remember)

Won't even get into my hair

(does snipping motion)

My friends called him "the crab"

    (pinches thigh, flashes teeth, crosses legs then uncrosses, brings knees to chin, rests chin on knees, is still, gets up, stretches fakely, stares blankly, heads toward door)

That dark green stop hitting yourself

Made a day of it

One day and then another. A pile of days

And their doors

♦

Gets out of car, removing the wallet from her purse

"Why couldn't we hear her?"

"She wasn't speaking"

A flower would listen

If you'd only drop

Your other eye

One of our favorite games was "prescription." How it worked was you told everyone what was wrong with you and they each wrote their "prescription" on a piece of paper without identifying who they were (no names, nicknames, inside jokes; handwriting had to be disguised, etc.) The papers were then crumpled and tossed into a bowl, which was handed to you, the patient, for mixing-up, and once that was done, you read them aloud one by one so you could pick the one you liked best. Then you slept with the prescriber.

◆

Sobbed into the apartment intercom.

I'm so glad to see you. You're going to let me see you, right?

                                                                          I do not dream.

He heard her / He hurt her / He heard her / He hurt her / He heard her / He hurt her

                                                                                He hurt her?

He heard her and he hurt her. And all time is shade

PROBLEMS IN WALKING AT NIGHT

He asked if he could buy my skirt—the one I was wearing

"They ding-dong ditched me, and now I have to drink myself to the door"

My voice was loud
A bit like a yard
I was envious of the cat; I dressed to be warm
And alone

♦

A friend will tell you it is difficult to be present
With most people
She *saw* his ear hear her

Later she scraped the bottom of her chin
On his belt

♦

A way to walk that tells, on the phone or off
That the voice collects in the foot
A day is a grain on a work
You are a work you care for yourself
The eye as always turns inward
For a look

I didn't like him because he interrupted a conversation I was having to ask if my tits were fake

That was merely diagnostic, he said later, breathing on my face

Like any reasonable person when I arrive at the counter, rapping on glass with my card

Boiling, I thought *I'll lift his face like a lid and take what's not rotted*

Rapt, I said *I'll keep you swaddled in the crease of my eye*

There is nothing done not a service, and when I get home I'm going to want something. I might later send it back.

A pillow as a mirror, or an office lodged in the face

Designed to keep you at all hours

clocked

What I recognize in a face is how I'm about to be treated.

The sun sets gorged on its errors, fat like a holiday. You bubble out of bed like a thought, curling into lift. At noon she's phoneless on a hill with a broken bell, bouncy from champagne. Pledging to be sick with the matter.

Apologized to the tree after I kicked it

♦

The head goes, the feet go   (the feet go, the phone goes)

♦

In a tunnel, I was dim but proud. Fog tended to the rest

♦

My keys, my typing eye

♦

Variously, real as tape. Breached by lip

♦

Love, my clicks—

♦

Saying this. And what will you drink

Asking what you care about

But the eyes stayed still and the head not turning

I have to walk so I can think. Drive to scheme

My glares: little bites on the finger so the finger remembers

Must everyday think herself up

He had a sad way of breaking things. He wouldn't really break them

And would go back later to finish

♦

In the car with my coat spread over my lap, I thought often of children

Runners in the park, ripping packets of gel with their teeth

Running is light living, brothy

I began to ask myself questions of business—how can the service offered be strengthened, where can time be trimmed?

I left blueprints and pie charts in strategic locations at key times, the first test being of course to see if he was marketable to himself

Awake to be tired

at which point you go home, and I take a rake to the clothes

GROMMET: AN ADDRESS

It was hot, and I'd forgotten we were talking

Became awake to your face awaiting reply

I said, *sorry, what did you say?*

You looked at the sky and I knew

It was my turn to speak

Keys under ice

        today's want: to still the buzzing eye

He's rarely in sleep, so the hope is he's there. Him in mind
     blurs   several rings

                No new thoughts, or I don't care to

            cry   parked and otherwise idle

No thing to be thought of, thin rings of mint thinning spit   ashy blanket

                Waiting for what won't to blow past

Waving my hand, I signal belief in what I've woken to

Sad, and so stands for sadness; lucky, and so recognized as your own

He asked for a story and I gave one: "I was eating ice cream at the shop when a girl I didn't know walked over and licked my cone"

                                                               "Licked your cone?"

Loving him is my country. I never got much out of a road

Walk because I desire the present, write to know what I think

But what did he mean "sworn?"

The ring around that cloud

My thin book recording not a word

♦

Sat on the face

And began to speak—swath of breathy trees

Wrestling on the bed when the paper becomes audible; he slides his hand into my back

pocket and recovers a note, smiles as he begins to open it. Stops his hands when

he catches my face.

He tries to play this off. "I thought I was being cute."

But still holding the folded up

list he fished from me. Not putting it down. Watching my eyes as his hand makes them boil

We rent a cabin for the weekend

The first night, we're having sex when he begins to cry—that I might leave him

Oddly, he doesn't stop while explaining, and we continue after I've reassured him,

though it doesn't seem our continuation hinges on my response

He appears more aroused than he did when we began, though it makes sense,

though he doesn't look at me, is scarcely keeping his eyes open (glassy white slivers)

When he cums, he looks unusually private—almost as if he's fucked himself

"I was imagining it as some kind of flowery disk, but it was not that at all"

"He opened the door for me, and it seemed a bit much, but then I felt feverish as we drove"

"We pulled up to what he had called a 'small recreational parade,' but to me it looked like a few dozen men and women, all beautiful, sitting in a circle as one read from a giant scroll"

"He seemed to know where I lived, though I hadn't told him, but I didn't question it"

"I went to sleep in the bed upstairs, still wearing my dress, and woke up on the couch in my underwear. He told me I sleepwalk and should probably see a doctor."

Disgust is fear's erotic response to anger.

He left some spit in a cup on the table and I almost drank it. Lost it.

When more than thirty-five text messages are sent to one recipient in less than ten minutes without reply, the sender's service is suspended for twenty-four hours.

Pulling down the bill of her cap, she lay back on the lounge and the orchids went white, blue, white again, pinkish bluish white, all absence of white, fizzing pinpricks making little pops nervy, filmy, nervy, speedy, grinning, filing, telling, dying, spinning, dying, pending, done. Breath of scalp.

Locks up the face while the owner's away.

A book on the highway, I did not swerve

♦

Mountains on my left   (later, my right—*how do I enter?*)

Papers flying in back   (strip of wind through my window)

A check for a head   (blank)

Sweetly borrowed noon, my scatter of books.

Whole pack of gum gone in twenty minutes.

TO PACK:

Clothes

Shoes

Books

Toiletries

Linens

Art

Furniture (?)

Appliances (?)

Misc.

Leave note

A book of lists

He dreamt he'd hung himself up in the basement, and was trying to cut his body down before I got home.

I dreamt a child dressed me in his clothes, walked without them into the snow.

Where exactly are you?

Anything put to music feels like living.

Sink of mouthy dishes, face fed with sun. My hand tracks

My eye

And where is your eye?

My love fills himself with saps and vapors, a brainy

Engine. Bits of rain catch his lashes and he tacks them above

His desk

Count down from thirty
Count down from sixty
Name sixty animals (use fingers)
Nouns that are red
Past boyfriends (name and one-word descriptor)
Top ten beverages, alcoholic
Top ten beverages, non-alcoholic
Dump out purse, reorganize
Your age in swipes of lip balm
What each button in the car does (in a sexy voice)
Your name, age, place of birth, occupation, and address
His name, age, place of birth, occupation, and address
Section eleven of the owner's manual out loud (anti-lock brakes)
Other words for "remove"
The first song you remember (sung in a whisper)
Story a mother might tell her son
Story a son might tell his mother
Get in the backseat and pretend the back of the driver's seat is him (until morning)

Your eyes were still on the sky　　(had they been the entire time?)

They looked alive but done:　　spit sliding down a window

　　　　Wanted

to speak, but I'd　　　　　　　　done that, had nothing

　　　　　　　　　　　　new or sharpened　　I shouldn't

touch you

　　　　　　　　　　　　　　　　　　　　Or was afraid to.

Imagined I was a flower. Flower births are asynchronous; the soul born immediately into the next life leaving the decoy body behind in an earlier version. We see it waiting to be pulled by its face from the ground

ACKNOWLEDGMENTS

Many thanks to the editors of the following publications where some of these poems originally appeared: *APARTMENT*, *Horse Less Review*, *Yalobusha Review*, *Twelfth House*, *TENDER LOIN*, and *Doubleback Review*. Other poems from this manuscript were included in the digital chapbook *Sour Candy*, published in 2018 as part of Really Serious Literature's Disappearing Chapbook Series.

Boundless gratitude to Julie Carr, Ruth Ellen Kocher, and Adam Bradley for reading this manuscript in its earlier versions and helping shape it toward its final form.

Thank you also to Juliana Sartor and Connor Fisher, friends whose unwavering support helped create the conditions in which it became possible for me to write this book.

Special thanks to my dear friend and co-editor Ray Levy for encouraging me to get over myself and release this book (and all else attached to it) into the world.

Finally, thank you to Kevin Barrett Kane for the gorgeous cover, and to Freddy La Force especially for publishing *TACT*, and for his warmth and vigor as an editor.

ABOUT THE AUTHOR

Lily Duffy is a poet, editor, and social worker living in Denver, Colorado. She is the author of *Wet Water Hill* (Garden-Door Press, 2021) and *Sour Candy* (Really Serious Literature, 2018). Duffy holds an MFA in Poetry from the University of Colorado Boulder and will soon graduate with her MSW from Metropolitan State University of Denver. She currently works with adults experiencing severe and persistent mental illness. With the writer Ray Levy, Duffy edits *DREGINALD*, an online magazine of poetry, prose, and art they founded together in 2013. *TACT* is her first full-length book.

www.ingramcontent.com/pod-product-compliance
Lightning Source LLC
Chambersburg PA
CBHW051807100526
44592CB00016B/2604